A Tree, a Human and a Robot.

By Jean-Pierre Murray-Kline

A man, a robot, and a tree walk into a bar... Wait, just joking.

This short book is a collection of three articles that I published in 2024, covering themes of Artificial Intelligence, Humanities, and Environmentalism. Like all my work, these pieces explore subjects that shape the trajectory of our society. "The Bedtime Story" is a fantastic read that reconnects the reader with nature. "Africa Colonized the World" tackles an emotional subject, encouraging introspection on a narrative shared among citizens. "The Mzansi AI Manual" provides an easy-to-understand and fascinating overview of everything you need to know about AI. Decision-makers both at home and office are attempting to navigate the challenges in South Africa. This book offers fresh insights and a new perspective on three major issues influencing our future. Please consider becoming a Change Champion and Future Thinker, enjoy the book!

TABLE OF CONTENTS.

PRELUDE.

The book cover photo is of me in a dry river valley in Rawsonville where I spent a weekend writing. I could have used a photo of my Google Home AI Bot and a Tree, but I wanted to take this opportunity to share the magnificent view of Mother Nature. It's an apt decision based on the bedtime story that you are about to read in this books first chapter.

A BEDTIME STORY.

Get a nice cup of hot chocolate and some Niknaks chips. Now curl up in bed and enjoy. This is the perfect story for the entire family, it is for young and old, the curious, business people, and scholars. The pages that follow are filled with interesting facts, a little bit of suspense, and perhaps even a touch of wonder. You will make a new friend, learn how life started, how it works, where you fit in, and where we might, as a species, one day end up. Today, we live in an age where our children are able to name more TikTok celebrities than plants in their garden, or where people live and work thinking they are not part of something important and truly miraculous.

A New Friend.

Dear Reader, I would like you to meet someone very important, and too often ignored: please meet "Mother Nature.". Perhaps you imagine her, or him, as jolly, plump, clever and a rather old character? The truth is we are part of Mother Nature, but we have forgotten this fact. True too, and perhaps less known, is that there is an undeniable link and remarkable similarity between nature and our own technology. It is a fact that many of the things we invent are recreations of Mother Nature's own work. There is so much we still don't know, but in spite of our own naivety, nature continues to influence our lives, homes, businesses, and even our works of art and the technology we are so proud of. Where do we start to learn about our new friend?

Perhaps with the Gaia Hypothesis? This idea proposes that the planet Earth is a super organism, and humans (and our technology) could be seen as a type of illness by the Earth's body. This supports the idea that global warming (like a virus) is the planet's way of running a fever to get rid of us, basically an autoimmune response.

I do not subscribe to the idea that the world has a higher consciousness and wants to be rid of us all, but we are definitely misbehaving enough to upset every section of the planet. What went wrong? Well, at some point we decided we are a supreme species, separate and above the environment. Why we did this is perhaps best answered by a psychologist, but nonetheless we have formed an ill fabricated perception of elevation above the ecosystem. We have a majesty complex. This has gone on for too long. We have developed a bogus reality and are mistakenly confident that our behaviors are acceptable. Modern humans no longer teach children how to be natural beings. We have in many ways regressed our mind-sets while trying to progress things like our economy and cities.

I won't deny the wonders of humans. Really, we are a wonder. We should all take a moment and look at some of the achievements we have made. We don't do this often enough, and a bit of self-reflection should be part of something all of us do, and try to avoid fixating on the negative. However, we must be mindful that there are many things other animals and plants do better than us.

If supremacy were based on lifespan, a species that has done well at actually living for a long time, then the red sea urchin would kick our butts because it is able to live for 200 years, or The Great Basin Bristlecone Pine, still alive today and about 5000 years old. Our global average lifespan is only about 73 years old.

There are scientists in Australia's national science agency who have created a genetic 'clock' computer model that estimates how long different vertebrates can survive based on DNA. They say humans have a maximum natural lifespan of 38 years. It is only because of our technology and innovation that we live longer.

With that said, we should be able to live up to about 120 years if we take into consideration the maximum number of times a human cell can divide (known as the Hayflick limit), which at a push is 60 times. So why don't we? Well, things like stress, pollution, and a bad diet don't help; I can tell you that much!

If omnipotence were judged in terms of population numbers, humans would lose here too. Bacteria come up tops with an estimated 4 nonillion (this is a real number and a lot more than a billion) alive in the Earth's ecosystem. There are so many of these microscopic critters that their biomass matches that of all the people on Earth, in spite of only weighing approximately 1 picogram each.

I think the only thing us humans can claim makes us 'better than other living things' is our intelligence, but then again, if we are so smart, why do we do so many harmful things? The runner-ups in the category for intelligence are Chimpanzees, Dolphins, Elephants, Crows, Ravens, Parrots, Mr. Octopus, and even Piggies. Many of these animals' attributes include high levels of memory, empathy, problem-solving skills, and advanced communication, and in some ways, they surpass us in these areas.

I subscribe to many of the points found in the theory of natural selection by Charles Darwin. A lot of what sparked his line of thought stemmed from a study of bird beaks on an island way back in 1859. In order to demonstrate and explain the relationship, link, and similarities between technology and nature — not only in the inventions of humankind but also through our tools, purpose, and execution — I first needed to delve into what nature actually is. This was a personal journey I undertook as a business and environmental technologist.

None of us can truly know ourselves without understanding Mother Nature. Understanding ecosystems is vital to comprehend just how nature reacts to mankind, our technology, and also our influence on Climate Change. At the time I started to write this chapter, I was reading a book by Stephen Hawking, in which he explains the rule of law of nature, which in many ways is worked out mathematically. I must admit, even after re-reading some of his points, I still do not fully understand all of his explanations. He was such a clever bloke.

What I, and you, can take from Stephen's book is that there are four primary theories covering energy/forces in our universe (observable and assumed), and there is an undeniable mathematical process in nature. Mother Nature is a remarkable Math and Science Teacher, if we actually attend her classes. Debates will continue (I hope), but I am content to know we have something called "M

Theory" which covers most of what we know, and that there is a very strong chance of our universe being one of many in the multiverse. Each and every universe (or version thereof) subscribes to the law of nature, which, by the way, can vary depending on the universe. (None exist where pineapple on pizza is okay.)

We very often build something using a concept nature invented during the process of evolution. There are countless examples of how we have copied or emulated nature to build machines. For example, the wings of a plane are styled from the wings of birds. Swarm Robotics is another.

Throughout the ages, we have been inspired by a desire to explore and understand; unfortunately, we do this through a looking glass of superiority. This creates a colossal problem. Ego and greed are characteristics humans have almost perfected. They have been so detrimental and harmful and can be found in just about any of our root causes of problems. We genuinely are convinced that we are the most important things alive. In our argument, we will share select scientific facts, and some will even use religion.

As a species, or even as the category of mammals, we are actually a minority. There are around 8.7 million types of animals and plants on Earth, and we discover new ones every day. Unfortunately, about 150 species of living things are estimated to become extinct every 24 hours. Please read that last sentence again. You can fact-check this point if it sounds too scary to be true. I want you to ask yourself how many of these species were affected by us and Human-induced (anthropogenic) Climate Change. The phrase ecocide really is an apt description of what is happening right now.

The way we have lived and worked to date is not sustainable, nor ethical. We need to find and pursue better ways to advance. No other creature seeks explanations more than we do; after all, when was the last time you heard a bird ask why the sky is blue or a fish how it can breathe underwater? It never happens. Our understanding of the environment is the reason humans became the dominant species on earth, but could also be the reason we destroy more than we build. We have a tremendous responsibility, and it's important to recognize our potential for good and bad.

Putting things in boxes.

Greek philosopher Aristotle was a forerunner in categorizing types of species, mainly by the way they gave birth. This I admit is an interesting approach to putting things into boxes. He declared that there are five levels of animal categories, and of course he placed man at the top. Today, when deciding on animal groups, we involve a field of biology called taxonomy. (This has nothing at all to do with tax. Humans are the only creature on earth that charge one another for things.)

Taxonomy is the science of naming, defining, and classifying organisms into groups based on shared characteristics. For example, the 'chief' taxonomic rank name is called Domain. This is all about cellular organization and genetics. There are three documented areas for 'Domains': Archaea, Bacteria, and Eukarya. I know this part of the story has some complicated words, but don't panic, you don't have to remember all of this, just be in awe of the diversity of life we have and the fact that we have had to come up with so many names.

Excluding humans, there are about 3 trillion plants on planet earth, 10 quintillion (10^19) insects, hundreds of billions of fish and also hundreds of billions of birds. Mammals, amphibians, and reptiles still need to be added to these numbers, but their category groups and numbers are less compared to bugs. Suffice to say, this planet has a lot of life!

Another taxonomic rank, and the one I use the most, is called the 'Animal Kingdom', which decides by organizing the critters based on fundamental traits. There are Animalia, Plantae, Fungi, Protista, Archaea, and Bacteria. Another one is when we categorize and sort by Phylum. This is all about body plan characteristics. An example would be Chordata which is a phylum that includes animals with a spinal cord. We could also sort by Class, Family, and Genus. Deciding on a group based on what organisms can interbreed is another way to group critters who might share some indifferent characteristics but can still produce offspring.

If you have met me in person, you will know I absolutely love my food, so I want to do things differently and group animals in the order of their food energy efficiency, basically what they eat and absorb. This is an important distinction because we don't actually absorb everything we put in our mouths. If we did, we would have none of that nasty stuff that comes out the other end, or certainly less. I am also not suggesting that this category puts creatures into an order of who poos the least, but if I were to pick a winner, it might have to be the Thorny Devil Lizard or perhaps even the Koala. Something odd I learned at a Games evening at the time I was writing this is that a wombat is known for producing cube-shaped poo. How odd! The hummingbird is known to be one of the animals that eats most frequently and Sloths the least.

Trophic levels are basically the spot a creature has in the food chain and also a great way to describe the flow of energy through an ecosystem. The flow is never linear but more of a web. We are talking about categorizing animals by energy efficiency. First, we have the Producers. These are plants and algae that produce their energy through photosynthesis. They gobble sunlight! Then we have the Primary Consumers (Herbivores) who eat Producers. Next are the Secondary Consumers (Carnivores); these animals eat Primary Consumers. They are followed by Tertiary Consumers who are also predators that feed on secondary consumers. Now things get a little dirty. Next up are Decomposers. These are creatures like fungi and bacteria that break down dead creatures and recycle nutrients back into the ground.

Out of these categories, who is the most energy-efficient? To answer this, we need to use an 'energy thermometer' measurement called trophic efficiency. Trophic efficiency is fascinating on its own, so let me quickly share a few nuggets on the subject.

Trophic efficiency is about the transfer of energy from one trophic level to the next in the natural food web. For example, Producers to Primary consumers, or let me put it another way: a Plant absorbs some sun, then a cow comes along and eats that plant, but then a human eats that cow, but the human dies a few days later and fungi and bacteria decompose the human. The 'energy thermometer' can help us work out how much of the sun's energy in that process actually got to the bacteria at the end.

The average is that about 10% of the energy moves from one trophic level to the next. There is a name given to this too: 'Lindeman's efficiency'. Humans love naming things!

Here is a working example of Lindeman's efficiency: if Producers (plants) capture 1000 units of energy from sunlight, only about 100 units will be available to primary consumers (herbivores). The next level will only get 10 units, the next 1, and the little bacteria, I think, is left with a very sad 0.10. (Don't feel bad for them; they are not very hungry critters anyway).

Understanding trophic efficiency helps ecologists work out the energy budgets in an ecosystem. I want to conclude this section of the story by explaining the ways living things actually obtain their energy from the bits and bobs they are eating. To do this, we also put things into categories through the process of Metabolic Classification.

Our classification, and all animals, are in the category called Heterotrophs. This is when we obtain both energy and carbon by eating organic (meat or vegetable) compounds. We need carbon because it is a foundational element in all living things molecules. Carbon is an element perfect for forming complex molecules necessary for life because of its brilliant bonding capabilities.

The second group is Photoautotrophs. This group likes to take selfies. Sorry, that is such a dad joke, this category is actually organisms like plants and cyanobacteria which use sunlight to produce energy and carbon compounds from carbon dioxide.

Finally, there is Chemoautotrophs organisms that obtain energy by oxidizing inorganic substances using CO2 as a carbon source. Did you see that rust on the car outside? That is literally 'life' having dinner using this process and obtaining some energy.

The very big family photo.

I study all things that influence our society and there is no university that offers this course. Everything I write about comes from unending hours of my time, which I have given in the pursuit of understanding why people do what they do and to try and share information that inspires people to try new ways of running their homes and businesses with a moral compass as its foundation.

To be part of the solution to the challenges we face, we cannot focus exclusively on making money, politics, or our own immediate family interests. I want you, dear Reader, to know that I have no university degree and all of this is done as my side hustle. I too have a business I run and a family to take care of. I will never tell people how to live and work, but hope to set an example that inspires people to see that there might actually be another and better way. There is a bigger picture.

The concept of an ecosystem has been around since the 1930s and ecology is probably one of the most diverse scientific fields with so many disciplines involved. To name a few: chemistry, geology, climatology, genetics, and the list goes on. One could say it is the 'M Theory' of studies. An ecosystem is a community of organisms interacting with each other and their physical environment. Humans are part of numerous ecosystems because we move about so much.

People are not the most important animal in any system. In fact, there isn't a single most important animal or plant in any given ecosystem because each species plays a unique role and is dependent on others for its very survival, but each system will have a few keystone species that are crucial and perhaps even unique to that system, and these species will play a prevailing role and have a significant influence on the overall ecosystem's structure and function. Some examples of such species are bees, wolves, elephants, and cute little sea otters.

As a Future Thinker and Change Champion, I study all things that influence nature, business, and our technology. I have identified one major hindrance in our progress in deciphering ecosystems and it is religion. This is especially evident in the Middle Ages where the notion of evolution was a taboo topic, with faith leaders who were adamant on teaching that everything was created by God, and that there was no mathematical or scientific involvement at all. Today, 'evolution' is still heavily contested by religious fanatics. I have personally been stopped by an elderly lady who managed to talk to me for almost an hour at a Mugg and Bean coffee shop. I must say, she was an excellent salesperson and if things were different I would have hired her for one of my businesses.

That day, she was peddling the notion that the Old Testament and the entire process of creation had taken place over a few days a couple of thousand years ago. She would not entertain any feedback from me that life might very well have started 4 billion years ago. There can be a middle ground between science and religion, and I don't see why they can't both exist. There have been some influential faith scholars. A good example is the monk Mendel, who in 1866 first recorded genetic inheritance, using vegetables (garden peas) in his own experiments.

Evolution has to do with the mutation of cells (which happens naturally through cell replication, or damage to cells through radiation or environmental factors), these mutations either improve or decrease the chances of survival. Today, every animal and plant has come from a line of ancestors which branched off in several directions.

I want to share the story of evolution based on the best available scientific information we have today. As I mentioned before, I write based on my research and I come across conflicting information from time to time, so this is my disclaimer that while there might be inaccuracies in some of my writings, they are for the most part spot on and based on the best available information I had on hand at the time of preparing my work.

We can track 'the first life' back to approximately 3.5-4 billion years ago using fossil evidence of single-celled organisms like archaea and bacteria. However, you would not have known these things were life even if they were sitting on the floor right in front of your eyes. Life as we commonly recognize was first evident around 550 million years ago in the sea. Plants came a little later, around 470 million years, and finally animals on land around 360 million years ago.

There is a scattered line of 'human' evolution starting around 2.8 million years ago, but 'people' as we recognize today (physically) only really appeared around 300 000 years ago. The evolution of 'us' was not simple and we almost became extinct around 74 000 years ago due to a natural disaster and a super volcano called Toba. I am fascinated by volcanos and I have climbed one between Rwanda and the Congo called Bisoke Mountain, and by the time you read this story would have also visited the largest active volcano in Europe called Mount Etna which is in Sicily in Italy.

I study natural disasters and I can tell you that life on Earth had to restart many times over because it experienced many extinction-level events which decimated entire ecosystems and changed global weather.

Every person today has a DNA lineage that includes DNA from a small group of people who survived the Toba disaster, their ancestors populated the rest of the world. We are literally all Africans, and an article written by me and worth reading is called 'Africa Colonized the World'. The choice to use the word

"Colonized" in the title is explained in the article. You can also find the addendum to the article called 'All About Us, the Information Pack', which offers a mind-blowing summary of the people of Africa, those who stayed, those who left, and those who came back again.

Way back in the old days, a lot of our understanding of ecosystems and evolution was determined through the study of food chains and fossils. As technology improved, our avenues to learn increased. Microscopes were one of the most useful technologies in the old days; unfortunately, there was no camera to record what was being viewed, and everything had to be hand-drawn. The recording and naming of species in the old days was a very important job.

DNA, in my opinion, was a pivotal discovery for humankind because it is something all living things have. It links us; it is the link, and it is the story of life. It is the equivalent of what we call Blockchain technology. The 'discovery' and concept that DNA carries genetic information happened over time, and scientists like Friedrich Miescher (in 1869), James Watson, and Francis Crick, and Rosalind Franklin all played a part (early 1950s) in the story of DNA. James and Crick made their announcement in the Eagle pub, claiming they had "discovered the secret of life". I assume most people just thought they were sloshed.

DNA stands for deoxyribonucleic acid. DNA sequencing is the process we use to compare the DNA of living things, using base pairs which resemble a barcode on a PC screen. There is a similarity of between 97% and 99% of our comparable DNA with great apes. Chimpanzees, Bonobos, Gorillas, and Orangutans are all genetic relatives of ours. Genuinely understanding this fact and accepting it should make you question the very meaning of 'what it is to be human'.

Scientists estimate that only a small percentage of our human genome (less than 25) contains genes that code for proteins. The remaining portion referred to as non-coding DNA or junk DNA has, as far as we can tell for now, only regulatory functions that we are still trying to understand.

As wonderful as we think our technology is, there is still more to learn than we already know. What is certain is that all living organisms share some degree of DNA similarity because of universal genetic code shared from evolutionary history. Ecosystem are family. All life on Earth is related; we are all children of Mother Nature and of this planet.

Who smells so smelly?

Deforestation became a real problem around 220 years ago, and we first started to understand the harm of greenhouse gases in the 1940s, a main factor contributing to climate change. We have known for a very long time how harmful our habits are. There are around 25 000 species at risk, and the majority of these are because of our farming practices. Land abuse and pollution of all sorts are killers. To play devil's advocate, one could say, "let the strongest species survive". But this would be very narrow-minded and to our own detriment considering the fact that The World Health Organization, or WHO for short, says air pollution is responsible for around 7 million people's premature deaths every year. That is a lot of people!

We need to consider the web of life and ecosystems in general. Bees pollinate about one-third of the veggies and fruit we chomp. Air pollution has significant negative effects on their navigation, health, reproduction, and overall habits. If they were to go extinct, what will soon follow within 3 to 6 months (my best estimate) would be a global ecosystem collapse, leading to mass starvation of our species and many others; subsequently, disease will follow, and then the extinction of mankind and many other animals and plants. This might sound like an exaggeration, but the truth is, it is an extremely probable outcome if humans didn't take extreme action to mitigate and find alternative solutions to the roles Bees play in our ecosystem. My point is, we need to Bee careful.

Many species of bees (of which there are about eight) are under threat from climate change, and a lot of their habitats are threatened by our cities. To protect all living things, we also have to protect the environment because an ecosystem is not just living things; it includes rocks, sunlight, and many other components. Survival of the fittest is a concept that works in the model of evolution, not environmental degradation by man on an accelerated and global scale that does not allow evolution to keep up. There is a difference between survival of the fittest (extinction of species that failed to adapt or evolve over a reasonable and natural period of time) and ecocide.

Sacrifice is built into ecosystems, for example, through the concept of 'kin selection'. This is when a living thing favors the reproductive success of a relative over its own life. Worker bees are excellent examples of this. Selective reproduction in nature might actually be part of its plan (it certainly has mathematical merit), and one could even entertain a debate that homosexuality is a type of natural population control. Homosexuality is found in many species. There are around 1500 documented types of mammals, birds, insects, and even some fish, making homosexuality perfectly natural.

A few quick nuggets: "Biotic" means living things. "Abiotic" means non-living things. An epiphyte is a plant that grows on another plant. "Citizen Science" is a real thing. Now that your brain is packed with a little more information, let's talk about your actual brain.

Our brain size, in proportion to our body, and when compared to other animals, is impressive. Our brain went through four major growth spurts, and there is evidence that these spurts happened during periods of time with high volcanic activity, leading to the theory that radiation around volcanic zones helped the evolutionary process.

A big brain likes to have tools. Most people are unaware that there are a variety of animal species that use apparatuses to help with tasks. Crows, elephants, dolphins, Mr Octopus, and chimpanzees are a few examples I can give. Chimps strip leaves off twigs to make sneers to dig bugs out of crevices in trees, or worse, to kill bush babies. (Chimps unfortunately share a number of unpleasant traits with us humans: they murder, kidnap, and steal.)

Sex in nature is not taboo. It is an essential mechanism, and without it, life may never have evolved to anything more than blobs of molecules. The first sexual "beings" we know emerged around 2.5 billion years ago, named "Isogamous" by biologists. Sex is information sharing.

Humans invented technology to transfer information in data files using computers. Nature does the same thing with encoded DNA, which is passed on during the reproduction process. A single gram of DNA is able to store about 215 million gigabytes of data. There is about 60 zettabytes of information in your body's cells. DNA defines us. It tells us how to grow an ear or breathe. DNA gives us instincts to help us find food or protect our children. It really is remarkable stuff!

Even species with the most advanced DNA need a variety of other beasts and plants within an ecosystem in order to survive. An ecosystem can have more than one stable state, but no system can maintain a state indefinitely, and ecosystems will always be in flux. Our DNA is also in a state of flux, always responding to influences. Each animal and plant present today is an upgrade from an earlier version but one that could not have developed without the external influences of the rest of the eco system.

Imagine for a moment trying to run Windows 11 on a PC from the year 2000, or vice versa. Each was perfect for its environment at the time but are highly inappropriate and unstable in each other's environments and networks. Another way to look at it, dinosaurs were powerful and mighty back in their day but would struggle in today's climate and environment. In order for new life to thrive, old life must cease.

Unfortunately, the pace at which life can evolve is limited by the sluggish speed of DNA progression, and that is why the global warming and climate change we are experiencing, which is substantially faster than normal, will be a death sentence for a lot of living things. Simply put, life cannot keep up.

Humans have harnessed the power to change the environment, and we don't need to wait for our biology to respond. This has given us a sense of dominion, but when you assess our position in the context of ethics, our ability to shape environments becomes a responsibility.

Life is clever energy.

Energy in a stable state and position is matter. Energy and matter cannot be created. It only changes form and position. "Life", from a particular point of view, could be defined as matter that can transfer energy and replicate itself. Life has the ability to manipulate the path of energy and the form of its own matter over time. 'Technology', by extension, is a primitive life form because it is also physical matter that transfers energy (electric data). Right now, the form and path of energy are determined by its creator (people), and it is not yet self-replicating or self-aware, but then neither was proto-life. Humans are working hard to create Artificial Intelligence. Soon we will have the first machine that will be able to replicate and evolve on its own.

Have you heard of the Kardashev Scale? The Kardashev Scale is a method of measuring a civilization's level of technological advancement based on the amount of energy they are able to use from their surroundings. If we could harness all the energy our sun releases over a period of a few days, we would have all the power we could possibly need for a very long time.

In the Kardashev Scale, type 1 is a species that can harness all the energy on its planet, including solar, thermal, volcanic, tectonic, and oceanic energy. Unfortunately, we fall short of this, and not because we don't have the technology, it is because we don't have the ethical will or commercial incentive. Type 2 can harness the power of its entire solar system and its star. This would be a superior species to us. Knowing what invention would be needed to achieve this is one of the ways some scientists are looking for aliens, by looking for the alien version of a machine we have called the "Dyson Swarm", which would be far easier to find because its size would exceed that of most planets. Type 3 can harness the power of all the stars and planets in their galaxy. Type 4, the power of all the suns and planets in their universe. There is a type 5, if you believe in the multiverse theory, and if this species existed, they would appear to have the power of God.

Life's history has been absolutely remarkable and has always involved the movement of energy and changes to the forms and shapes of matter. When energy stops moving, life dies.

The first beginning.

The universe is probably a little older than 13.8 billion years. Around 200 million years after its birth, stars were born (with gravity compressing matter), and within them, new elements were made through the process of nuclear fusion. Earth itself is about 4.54 billion years old. Our solar system (the space where our planets live around our sun) at the time of its infancy, was a lot of dust and gas made up of wet and dry particles. Generally speaking, particles within our system dispersed based on their liquid content.

Particles collided, and many stuck to one another. Over a lot of time, these blobs of mass became very large and formed planetesimals. Planetesimals spent many years smashing into one another, and those that combined grew into planets and moons. Planets spent more time colliding with one another as well, and that is how our moon was formed, which involved a Mars-sized planet colliding with (back then) a smaller Earth. The majority of debris helped grow our planet's size. The remaining bits formed our orbiting moon.

The most recent additions to orbiting objects around our planet are 3300+ active satellites, but we have also created a lot of space junk (broken satellites and fragments of rockets). There are about 34 000 pieces of debris larger than 10 centimeters and 900 000 pieces between 1 and 10 centimeters. It's a massive problem, and if we are not careful, it's going to be hard to leave the planet because you will inevitably crash into something and undoubtedly blow up and die. Have you heard of Space-Track.org? You can use this resource to monitor what is above our heads right now. I digressed, let's get back on track and down to planets.

There are eight "classic" planets and five dwarf planets in our solar system. There are arguments amongst clever people for a 9th planet and strong opinions on as much as 20 planetesimals.

Most planets are believed to have all formed more or less the same time, which was not long after our sun was born. It is believed that Earth is one of the youngest planets, and Jupiter is the oldest (in our solar system). During its toddler years, our planet and moon continued to be bombarded by planetesimals, and these helped create the atmosphere and ocean on Earth around 4.3 billion years ago. Eventually, we had our first rains, and with it, came erosion.

The land and ocean back then were hostile. The sea had a layer of CO2 floating above an H2O layer. Around 4.2 billion years ago, our planet had a liquid core, and from this, our Earth's magnetic field was born. Deep within our planet, you will find its mantle, which is normally the bulkiest part of most planets. The mantle forced heated rock upwards, and that pushed the crust (hard plates of colder rock) apart. This was the start of plate tectonics. Where the plates split, hot magma oozed up and formed new crusts, like blood in a wound creating a scab. At the same time, some parts of the crust were forced down, sinking back into the core of the Earth where they re-melted.

Back then (around 4.2 billion years ago), Earth was a slow cooker, with cooler matter sinking, and warmer matter rising. This cycle helped the ocean become less toxic by moving some of the chemicals into the Earth's core. For those of you who didn't know, life did not start on the planet's surface. It is believed that primitive life started within geysers inside the Earth's crust, which recycled hot liquids between the heated core and the cooler surface. Within this system, there was an abundance of uranium ore which emitted large amounts of radiation, and that helped create a range of materials, including the early building blocks of life, like amino acid (a group of organic compounds that form the building blocks of proteins and make up about 75% of our body). In many ways, all the stuff that makes us is extremely old, we are all very old matter.

The mixing of wet and dry cycles helped prota-RNA develop, which are life-encoding molecules. These, in turn, evolved into Ribozyme molecules (probably around 4.1 billion years ago), and they were something special because they were able to replicate themselves. RNA molecules have the power to catalyze specific biochemical reactions, including RNA splicing in gene expression. Still, we had not reached "life" as yet; we had only achieved "goo" status, which in the right environment, could make more goo.

More time passed, and eventually, the second stage of proto-life evolved. It used the sun to obtain energy for itself, and therefore the first type of primitive metabolism appeared. Sweet! Sugar could now be made to offer energy at night, and this meant 'life' could migrate away from the spaces where it used to get all their energy, which up until then, had originated from the core of the planet.

It is because 'primitive plant goo' managed to produce sugar glucose through the process of photosynthesis which converted carbon dioxide (of which there was a lot at the time) and water into glucose and oxygen using energy from the sun. This in itself was a miracle, and for those of you who want to know what the chemical equation for photosynthesis looks like, this is it: $[6CO_2 + 6H_2O + \text{light} \rightarrow C_6H_{12}O_6 + 6O_2]$. The next time you look at a plant and think it's not very clever, try to remember that it's calculating this equation.

Our bodies can perform some very complicated science math as well. An example would be oxidative phosphorylation, which takes place in our mitochondria (think of them as the 'power station' of cells), and the process is crucial for making adenosine triphosphate which we could call the 'energy currency' for our body's cells, which is needed to trade energy to other parts of our body and stay alive.

Let's get back on track and continue with the assumption that lots of chemical reactions and math was taking place. The earth's surface up until this point really was not pleasant, inimical in fact. This is a good time in the story to plot out some of the planet's mass extinction events which took place.

The first one happened around 443 million years ago, and we have called it the Ordovician-Silurian Extinction, during which the earth suffered the loss of many of its marine species. Its causes were probably from rapid Climate Change and a gamma-Ray Burst. It would have had devastating effects for life on earth.

We endured four more over time; the next was the Late Devonian Extinction around 359 million years ago probably caused by anoxia (lack of oxygen in the oceans), volcanic activity, and meteorites. Following that was the Permian-Triassic Extinction around 252 million years ago, and we also call this time in history "The Great Dying". During this period, approximately 90% of our marine species and 70% of terrestrial vertebrate species died, which made this extinction period one of the very worst ever. The reasons were probably caused by massive volcanism, Climate Change, methane release, and anoxia.

Then around 201 million years ago, we had the Triassic-Jurassic Extinction which negatively affected amphibians and some reptiles. The likely reasons this time were volcanic activity, Climate Change, and ocean acidification. The most famous one happened around 66 million years ago and is called the Cretaceous-Paleogene Extinction, and this is when we lost all the dinosaurs. Reasons were an asteroid impact, volcanism, followed by Climate Change.

Today, we are undergoing a sixth mass extinction-level event, and compared to all the prior ones, it is the most unnatural and probably the only one we could have avoided. It is in short a human-induced global crisis from habitat destruction, overexploitation, pollution, invasive species, diseases and of course, we cannot forget and not mention human prompted Climate Change because of excessive greenhouse gases.

Let's get back on track, we were discussing life around 3.8 billion years ago before any of the above-mentioned disasters took place. Life's unstable RNA would evolve (probably through ionizing radiation) into more durable DNA. This meant it was now possible to pass information onto the next generation of goo, which then brought us to the third type of proto-life, the beginning of prokaryotic organisms: the ancestors of today's bacteria. It is my opinion that this was the moment 'LIFE' was born. Instead of these masses of goo molecules just being able to replicate more of themselves, the new goo could now 'save' and 'update' information on changes it had made (through mutation), and then replicate the new design. Each generation was now a little wiser and better than the one that had come before. This was the birth of 'storytelling', an absolute universal heritage of all living things, life is storytelling, and here I am telling you a story about it!

Life's next magic trick would be to evolve and use oxygen as part of its process to create energy. Up until then, can you believe it, oxygen on Earth had actually been harmful to organisms?

Cyanobacteria (a blue-green algae) which first appeared around 2.4 billion years ago, produced oxygen and reduced iron content in the ocean. It was around this time that Earth went through a phase where mantel plumes created large landmasses which the cyanobacteria absolutely loved, and their numbers boomed. With that, oxygen levels rose substantially because these critters created it as a by-product. It was around this time that our oceans turned blue and the earth went through a Great Oxidation Event.

Unfortunately, around 2.3 billion years ago there was a collision between the Milky Way (our galaxy) and another smaller galaxy. During this cosmic pileup, many new stars were created. Some of these died in supernova explosions which bombarded our planet's solar system with so much energy our sun's heliosphere (a bubble of protection around all the planets in our solar system) deteriorated and Earth was abused by extreme cosmic rays. This radiation caused a chain of events, and Earth reacted by covering itself with clouds that would have blocked sunlight and devastated life. Our planet would have looked like a snowball from space. Fortunately, some life survived, and over time, the planet recovered.

Side nugget: our Milky Way galaxy has had several collisions leading to mergers with other galaxies throughout its existence.

Prokaryotes (unicellular organisms that lack organelles or other internal membrane-bound structures) evolved into more complex life, like endosymbiotic systems (blobs that lived within one another, without consuming each other) and had a mutually beneficial relationship of sorts. These creatures in turn evolved into mitochondria (a name I first learned from Star Trek) and chloroplasts.

Around 1.9 billion years ago, there was a very large landmass we have named Nuna. It provided wonderful habitats for bacteria, and without it, evolution may have been stunted. Life on Nuna flourished and increased atmospheric oxygen levels further. Eventually, over many more years, Nuna broke up, and its parts shifted around the globe, finally rejoining to create a new landmass called Rodina. We have had a variety of supercontinents over time: Pannotia, Pangaea, and Gondwana (which was actually half of Pangaea), along with a northern supercontinent known as Laurasia.

A large nugget: Obviously, the land we walk on is not the land that the earth first formed because of the cycling of supercontinents and many other geological processes over millions of years. With that said, there is a patch of land which has remained unchanged for almost the full life of the earth, and guess what South Africans, some of it is in your country!

The oldest parts of the Earth's crust are found in regions known as cratons. One of the most well-known cratons is the Kaapvaal Craton in southern Africa and the Pilbara Craton in Western Australia. Some of the rocks in these cratons have been dated to around 3.5 to 4 billion years old. If you want to find the oldest part of the earth's 'skin', the Acasta Gneiss in northwestern Canada is believed to be the oldest known part of our earth's continental crust, where zircon minerals found there were dated at about 4.02 billion years old.

Back to the story. While landmasses were shifting about, lots of chemistry and math was happening, and goo was getting more complicated and clever, there was a moment where collaborating cells evolved to become the first animals, and there is DNA evidence suggesting this happened around 800 million years ago. All living things (animals and plants) are classified as "multicellular eukaryotes." You, dear Reader, are a multicellular eukaryote from earth. I double dare you to address someone as that in the next email you send.

We are all part of one planet and children of the same lineage. I know some of us look very different, but that's just because life has played its toll on our DNA over hundreds of millions of years.

One very strange multicellular eukaryote cousin of ours is Mr. Octopus. They are very unique compared to any other animal because they can change their own RNA, and the fact that they have no backbone means they leave very few fossils, which made it nearly impossible to determine how old their species might be. This has resulted in some scientists suggesting they are extraterrestrial and they might have arrived on a comet. Supporting this concept is other evidence that suggests the evolutionary process of the octopus started at a different point in time.

The genome of the octopus shows a staggering level of complexity with 33 000 protein-coding genes. (We only have about 20 000). In addition to this, this animal has nine brains, blue blood, and 3 hearts. The male sex organ is on one of their arms, and the female's is in her head, through what appears to me (in diagrams) to be the equivalent of her nostril. The next time you look at one of them, you might actually be looking at the child of another far-off planet, which found its home here. It's a slim chance, but a possibility! How interesting is that?

Planet Earth itself is of course just one ecosystem of many of Mother Nature's ecosystems. There is a much, much bigger picture we are part of. The Milky Way galaxy is home to our planet's solar system, but there is an estimated 100 billion stars in the Milky Way, all of which have orbiting planets and their own solar systems.

The Milky Way is expected to crash into a larger galaxy called Andromeda in 4.5 billion years' time. Sounds scary? You don't need to worry at all; earth coming near to even one of these other planets or stars is extremely unlikely because there is so much space between us. Did you know that you can already fit every planet in our solar system between Earth and our own moon? It's true.

Andromeda and is about 110 000 light-years in size. Our galaxy is 52 850 light-years in size. The largest galaxy we know of is IC 1101; it is around 50 times the size of the Milky Way. Did you know there are suns out there that are huge! I mean absolutely colossal. Google "UY Scuti." It has a diameter of 2.37 billion kms, while our sun is only 1 392 000 kms in diameter.

Back to earth we go, and Mother Nature's story of life on our planet. Over more time, the continents started to sink, and the plates cooled the Earth's core. The cooling planet resulted in the loss of the Earth's dipole magnetic field (a magnetic force that emanates from two opposite poles) and a weaker magnetic field formed called a quadrupole magnetic field (four equal monopoles, or two equal dipoles close to one another with an alternating polarity).

Having a magnetic field back then, as is the case today, is the difference between having a planet like Earth and a planet like Mars. Mars lost its magnetic field around 4 billion years ago, and it is extremely inhospitable to life because of this. In short, magnets are good for life!

About 700 million years ago, the Milky Way collided again with another dwarf galaxy. More stars, more cosmic rays, clouds, and cold. This period of time was dubbed the "starburst period". The Earth, as it had done a few times before already, took some time to thaw out.

All these types of cycles repeated several times in our planet's history, and each time there was a major loss of life as a result. The planetary ripple effects included frequent fluctuating oxygen and radiation levels, which helped accelerate the evolution of many species while decimating others. Regardless life managed to grow from goo in a hole to goo in water, to primitive plant and critter moving onto land, finally onto the first group of species to dominate land. Amphibians, then reptiles, dinosaurs, mammals, and now us. Animals took to the sky between the reptile and the dinosaur eras.

The landmass called Pangea is where our very first ancestors first appeared at the rift of the Gondwana supercontinent. There were three types of primates: Old World, New World, and Lorises.

600 million years ago, our dipole magnetic field returned while the Earth's inner core cooled more. At the same time, our ocean levels dropped through a process called the 'leaking Earth phenomenon'. As a result, land surfaces increased, and more rivers formed, which were great for the mixing up of nutrients that life really enjoyed gobbling on.

It was now time for the Cambrian Explosion, a period when fossil records for complex animals began appearing. During this period, 35 new phyla evolved and became the foundation of the plants and animals we see today. Phyla make up a far more complex level of categories above the one we call the 'Kingdoms' for plants and animals, of which there are only 6 (plants, animals, protists, fungi, archaebacteria, and eubacteria).

Dear Reader, I want you to take a moment now please to reflect on just how much life has had to go through to even get to this point and appreciate that it really is a miracle you are alive today. The chances of someone like you being alive, reading this story, on a digital device humans have invented, which required life needing to learn the secrets of life itself and all the maths and sciences we have, could never ever be quantified.

Evolutions end.

We already know evolution is technically a very complex thing to take place, but it could be simplified into a handful of types of events. In this story, I want to summarize these for you because it's helpful to know why and how we have so many differences and the processes that shaped them.

Convergent Evolution is where a species with a similar function or feature to that of another develops, but it evolved independently and away from one another. Divergent Evolution is where two groups of the same species evolve different traits within the groups in order to adapt to different environmental or social pressures. Parallel Evolution is where there are geographically separated groups that evolve away from one another but still show morphological similarities.

The two "family events" of evolution are: Stem Evolution, which is what happens where continental rifts form and land masses move apart. Then there is Crown Evolution, which is what takes place where landmasses join again and species crossbreed.

The final part of this story includes Earth having yet another cold glacier period which was caused by the ripple effects of a faraway collision of a dark nebula, and its cosmic rays hitting our planet.

Space and the greater universe influenced life on earth a lot! There was a loss of plants, reduced oxygen, and with that, the death of many species. Those that did survive then had to deal with a meteorite estimated to be around 10 km wide in diameter, which rammed into Earth and sealed the fate for just about everything that was still alive. This is what wiped out the dinosaurs, and you now know to be one of the mass extinction events I have already written about in this story.

Mammals emerged successfully from this disaster because they were the most resilient creatures at the time. They then spent many years evolving into a number of animal species, one of which was primates who are believed to have first appeared around 55 million years ago. Our time finally arrived. We have reached the Humanozoic era.

Hominins appeared around 6 million years ago. Over time, we learned how to talk, we became self-aware, developed advanced memory and imagination. We worked on improving ourselves throughout the Pliocene era and well into the Holocene era.

Between 300 000 and perhaps as early as 1.2 million years ago, people left Africa on foot and migrated all over the world. What we know for certain is that around 200 000 years ago, ancestors of ours could be found almost everywhere. 100 000 years ago, we started the Agricultural Revolution. 5 000 years ago, the trade revolution. And with that, we developed cities, laws, and founded religions. Only 300 years ago, the Industrial Revolution was started in the United Kingdom. Around 35 years ago, the Information Revolution started with computers and the internet, birthing Industry 4.0.

I want to ask the Reader now a question about the serious problems of today, be it Racism or Inequality or even Climate Change. If you were to give these issues a time stamp percentage in the history of life, what percentage would it form?

I want us to appreciate that we heading towards a "unified nation period," and I hope whoever writes about us in the future has something really nice to say. If your packet of Niknaks has lasted this long, you have more control than me. I hope you have enjoyed this story, learned something new and have gained a sense of wonder and appreciation of your new friend Mother Nature and yourself. As a Future

Thinker, it would be silly of me to miss the opportunity to share a quick peek into our far future.

The Future

I believe we will change our type of fuels. Population growth patterns will reduce as we control our reproduction rate. The locations we inhabit will shift dramatically. Unfortunately while this is all happening there will still be periods of time with extreme food shortages and billions of refugees, a lot of hunger, and illnesses. There will be political, religious and civil unrest, and we will either reduce or increase the inequality gap. The way we trade, what we believe, and how we see one another will change. Natural and man-made disasters will increase in severity and frequency.

If we finally learn our lesson — that we are part of an ecosystem — and work together as one species, we will reprioritize and become true guardians of the planet. We must be Mother Nature. We, and the rest of life, can then endure.

One day we may leave the planet to become a spacefaring species. It might not be how we imagine it to be. It is probable we will only send our personal consciousness via AI onto far distant planets, rather than physically traveling there.

As for the planet Earth, it is predicted that in 200 million years' time, the continents on Earth will join again, CO2 levels will drop, many plants and animals will die, plate tectonic movements will stop, and the Earth's magnetic field will disappear. The atmosphere will dissipate, and all life on the planet will die. 1.5 billion years later, the oceans will be gone, and the Earth's average temperature will be around 500 degrees Celsius. 4 billion years onwards, our Sun gets old, expanding so much that it consumes our dead rock of a planet, and every trace of life on Earth will be gone. The life of the universe will succumb to a Big Freeze, the Big Crunch, or Big Rip.

Unless...

AFRICA COLONIZED THE WORLD.

I use social media from time to time as a thermometer on the moral temperature of society. I find this an exceptional and authentic firsthand tool as a writer. In one such instance, I posted the following on my social media thread:

"I am going to say something now that will upset some people and their beliefs, but it's true nonetheless. AFRICA COLONIZED THE WORLD. All of our species traveled from Africa. (Some returned a little later on boats and with an ego, but still, even Europeans come from Africa)."

In response to this, I got a few likes, a few people agreeing with me, and then there was Lorenzo van Schalkwyk (from Hermanus and now living in Germany) objecting. I have shared the screenshots of his objection on the online version of this article which you can find on my website. I do not write to preach to the converted. I write almost exclusively to those who might object. I want people to think alternatively about matters that influence society and our social fabric if the general narrative is being used for harm. From the feedback, I get insight into other people's points of view, and on really good days, they might even share some facts I was unaware of. (Unfortunately, Lorenzo didn't really offer those). I did invite Lorenzo to a Zoom chat, which he never accepted. I wish he had, he was for so many reasons an ideal person to engage with on this subject. If he had, this is what I might have hoped to cover:

I believe the first sentence in my post is self-explanatory, so let's skip to what I meant by "AFRICA COLONIZED THE WORLD." The word "Africa" for the purpose of the post meant people who have a heritage from Africa. "Colonized" I meant the practice of a country or group of people taking control of foreign land. This has often been done by force, technology, and sometimes even religion has been used. During this 'process' there is exploitation of people residing in that land, and they succumb to awful mistreatment, either because of 'lesser' technology to defend themselves, or perhaps they are literally a 'friendlier people' compared to the colonizers.

So the question you should have now is how on earth could I make such an absurd claim that the people of Africa colonized the world! (If that is what you were thinking, then my post worked)

The popular narrative is that Africa was colonized by Europeans. Spain, Italy, Portugal, Belgium, Germany, France, and Britain all had their turns. These are some of the nations I am referring to in the post with the text "… some returned a little later on boats and with an ego...". The word "ego" which I use in the same sentence should be understood to summarize the many awful things people from these nations did; some of their actions are documented, but even those records are not given the attention they deserve. I do write about these subjects, and a good article to start with is the one I called THE ARROGANCE, which you can read on my website www.jeanpierremurraykline.co.za

Let's not digress from the point of this article.

In South Africa, the narrative is that Europeans colonized Africa. What I will explain now is that there would have been no Europeans at all without Africans, and that Europeans and indeed all human races as we know them today have their heritage from Africa. To do this, let me ask and answer the following questions:

• What scientific evidence is there that all humans alive today are from Africa?

• Do all Caucasian people have DNA from Africa?

• Is there proof that people (of the same genetic lineage) left Africa, went to Europe, and then came back and colonized African land where other people were living?

The answer to the first question is where I would like to discuss the theory known as the "Out of Africa Theory," and it is supported by a substantial base of scientific evidence covering multiple disciplines. Let me share some points:

1. Fossil Evidence. Archaeological discoveries unearthed Homo sapiens fossils in Africa that date back to between 200,000 and 300,000 years ago. I believe some of the most prominent findings include the fossils from Jebel Irhoud in Morocco and Omo Kibish in Ethiopia. These sites contain the oldest known remains of modern humans.

2. There is Genetic Evidence. DNA is a great storyteller, and analysis has provided critical insights into human evolution. Vast studies of mitochondrial DNA (which is passed from mother to child) and Y-chromosome DNA (passed from father to son) reveal that all living humans can trace their ancestry to a single population in Africa. How amazing is that! This is an epic fact none of us should ever forget and should be used to unite us, not to divide.

3. Migration Patterns. Humans are actually very well designed when it comes to walking. Reputable studies say that between 60,000 to 70,000 years ago, a small group of us humans migrated out of Africa and spread across the rest of the world. We did this on foot and on animals. This very long migration led to the establishment of populations in Europe, Oceania, Asia, and the Americas. Humans are messy, and we have left all sorts of artifacts such as tools, weapons, and even our skeletons along the path.

4. A more interesting tell sign. Cultural and Technological Evidence from archaeological findings of early human artworks and other cultural artifacts support the African Origin Theory. Very early 'sophisticated' tools and art have primarily been found in Africa, and similar technologies later appeared in Europe and Asia. This confirms a spread of innovation (and stories) following the migration path out of Africa.

5. Then there is Paleontology and Comparative Anatomy. This is about the study of early hominid fossils showing a gradual development of features that are characteristic of us modern humans. The earliest hominin species, such as the Australopithecus and the very early Homo species, are found exclusively in Africa. This proves that the evolutionary lineage leading to the Homo sapiens of today is rooted in the African continent. (Africa the continent is about 180 million years old.)

To answer the next question, 'Do Caucasian people, like all humans, have DNA that traces back to Africa?'

1. The Common Ancestry fact. Genetic evidence consistently shows that all modern humans, regardless of race, share a common ancestry in Africa. This is based on mitochondrial DNA, as I mentioned in my prior answer. These genetic markers confirm a lineage that traces back to a small population of early Homo sapiens who lived in Africa around 200,000 to 300,000 years ago. There was also a point in time when humans as we know it had a population bottleneck due to a natural disaster which brought our numbers down to between 3,000 to 10,000 individuals. We almost went extinct. This probably happened because of the Toba Catastrophe, and that is a subject well

worth learning more about too. The point is, everyone alive today has genetic markers (and ancestors) from that small population which remained only 74,000 years ago. Not only are we all related, but we are not as distantly related as we think.

2. Interbreeding with other Hominins. Yes, we did this. While migrating, early modern humans interbred with other hominins such as the Neanderthals and the Denisovans. Neanderthals and Denisovans are 'sort of human' but from another branch of the evolutionary tree, but still genetically very similar. (Obviously, or we would not have been able to have babies). These other 'sorts of humans' died out. Why? That's a subject for another article, but what is important to remember is that these other 'sorts of humans' also evolved from people from Africa, but they left the continent between 200,000 to 300,000 years ago. These 'affairs' between 'them' and 'us' contributed to the genetic makeup of present-day Caucasians, but the initial genetic heritage still traces back to Africa.

The final question. 'Is there proof that people (of the same genetic lineage) left Africa, went to Europe, and then came back and colonized African land where other people were living.' Yes, answered above, and they were all African!

To conclude: Africa colonized the World. Europeans are also African. It was Africans that colonized the World, including Africa. This is a fact you have to accept if you consider the bigger picture and all the available facts, not just a limited recording of history by humans over the most recent 5,000-year period. It might also be of interest to know that while modern African countries did not engage in 'colonization' in the same manner as Europeans did during the 'Age of Exploration' or the 'Scramble for Africa', there were African empires, tribes, and kingdoms that wielded control over vast territories and engaged in conquests and expansion. Lots of nasty things happened during these invasions of territory.

All animals try to excel. It is unfortunate there have to be victims, but it appears to be the evolutionary process of making a species stronger.

Dear reader, I wrote this article not to stir racial tensions, but to remind everyone that we are all human, all from the same planet, all imperfect and all related. All humans have been tribal and all humans have hurt one another. In 2024, it is not always constructive arguing about who was where first and who owns the land. That is the point of my post, to offer an alternative but factually true point of view which should nullify a common argument in South Africa today. The concept of ownership and entitlement is something we perpetuate, and it is how we ended up with victims to start with. To succeed, let's drop the ego.

The End.

Would you like to know more? Perhaps:

- Who arrived in South Africa first, Europeans or Zulus?
- What was the order of inhabitants of Africa all time?
- If the Xhosas 'arrived' before the Zulus?
- What was the early migrations within and out of Africa, and then of course back again?

Keep reading then dear Reader.

ABOUT US ALL.

An Information Pack

This is a mind-blowing summary of the people of Africa, those who stayed, those who left, and those who came back again. Before you start, please be aware, and accept that the history of us humans and our habitation in Africa spans millions of years and includes a varied range of hominin species and modern human cultures. It is nearly impossible to provide a conclusive "order" because of overlapping timelines, but this summary uses information which is for the most part the most widely and acceptable records of facts. One thing is for certain, is gosh we liked to move around a lot!

The beginning! (Information Pack prelude)

Let's bullet point this.

1. The Early Hominins

- The Australopithecus (*around 4 to 2 million years ago*): One of the earliest known hominin genera. Famous specimens like "Lucy" (Australopithecus afarensis) were discovered in East Africa. Evidence of them at least!
- The Paranthropus (*around 2.7 to 1.2 million years ago*): Robust hominins that coexisted with early Homo species.
- The Homo habilis (*around 2.4 to 1.4 million years ago*): An early member of the genus Homo, known for using simple stone tools.

2. Then the Early Homo Species

- Homo erectus (*around 1.9 million to 110,000 years ago*): they are known for more advanced tools and control of fire, with fossils found across Africa and Eurasia.
- Homo heidelbergensis (*around 600,000 to 200,000 years ago*): They are considered a common ancestor of both Neanderthals and modern humans, with remains found in various African sites.

(FYI: the word "homo" means "same")

3. Next are the Anatomically (Starting to look a little like us) Modern Humans

- Homo sapiens (*around 300,000 years ago to present*): Modern humans first appeared in Africa. The early Homo sapiens fossils have been found in sites like Jebel Irhoud (in Morocco) and Omo Kibish (in Ethiopia).
- Finally, someone we know! The San and Khoikhoi (Khoisan peoples) (*one of the oldest continuous populations still alive today*): The genetic evidence suggests that they are among the earliest diverging lineages of modern humans.

4. The Ancient African Civilizations

Civilizations can be easily identified by language and therefore our voice and words are wonderful tools in literally telling our story. We are the only species on earth who record our stories with art and writing.

- The Nilo-Saharan and Afro-Asiatic speakers: These language groups spread and settled in various parts of Africa, contributing to the development of early civilizations.
- The Ancient Egyptian Civilization (*around 3100 BCE to 30 BCE*): They were located along the Nile River, it is one of the world's earliest and most influential civilizations.

- The Nok Culture (*around 1000 BCE to 300 CE*): They were known for their advanced terracotta sculptures in West Africa (the modern-day Nigeria).

5. Our Bantu Expansion

- The Bantu-speaking peoples (*around 3000 BCE to 1000 CE*): Originating from the region of modern-day Cameroon and Nigeria, Bantu-speaking groups spread across large parts of sub-Saharan Africa, bringing with them agriculture, ironworking, and many new social structures.

6. Later African Kingdoms and Empires

- The Kingdom of Nubia (including Kerma, Napata, and Meroë) (*around 2300 BCE to 350 CE*): was well known for its culture and interactions with Ancient Egypt.
- The Ghana Empire (*around 300 to 1200 CE*): They were a powerful West African kingdom known for its wealth and trade networks.
- The Mali Empire (*around 1235 to 1600 CE*): They were famous for its powerful rulers like Mansa Musa. It is also where the city of Timbuktu came from!
- Great Zimbabwe (*around 1100 to 1450 CE*): It use to be known for its impressive stone structures and role in trade networks. (It makes me sad to see the status of this once great nation is today)

7. Finally we are at the Colonial and Modern Periods

- The Colonial Era (*late 19th century to mid-20th century*): Following the Berlin Conference (1884-1885), European powers colonized and controlled much of Africa.

- Post-Colonial Period (*mid-20th century to present*): Period marked by the struggle for independence and the formation of modern African nations.

Questions to the Reader:

It would appear that there is something in common in all 'tribes' throughout our full history: we like to move about, expand and whenever possible dominate extra territory. As time progressed, weaponry improved but not at an equal pace per 'tribe'. As one 'tribe' became stronger, was colonisation not eventually inevitable by one tribe or another? Could history have played out another way with other victors and other victims?

Who arrived in South Africa First, Europeans or Zulus?

This is a loaded question and of much debate today. The history of human settlement in South Africa is extremely complex and involves various groups arriving at different times. It's a very emotional topic. I also need to point out that South Africa is not really the cradle of mankind, in spite of a certain 'tourism' spot we have. The earliest humans (Homo sapiens) are believed to have come from East Africa, predominantly along the East African Rift Valley.

Let's get on with the answer.

I will bullet point some facts and then offer a conclusion.

Bantu Expansion and the Arrival of the Zulus

2. The Bantu-speaking Peoples:
    o   Starting around 2,000 years ago, Bantu-speaking peoples began migrating into southern Africa from the north. These groups brought with them agricultural practices and ironworking skills. They gradually moved southward, displacing or assimilating Khoisan groups.
    o   By the 16th and 17th centuries, many Bantu-speaking communities had established themselves in various parts of South Africa, including the area that would become the Zulu Kingdom as we know today.

3. The Zulu People:
    - o The Zulu are part of the larger Nguni ethnic group and are Bantu-speaking people. The Zulu nation as a distinct entity was formed in the early 19th century under the leadership of King Shaka Zulu. By this time, various Nguni groups, including the ancestors of the Zulu, had been in the region for several centuries.

Now, onto the arrival of Europeans (Europeans as we know them today).

4. The European Arrival:
    - o The Portuguese Explorers: The first Europeans to reach the southern tip of Africa were Portuguese explorers in the late 15th century. Mr Bartholomeu Dias rounded the Cape of Good Hope in 1488, and Vasco da Gama later reached the Indian Ocean in 1497.
    - o Dutch Colonization: The first significant European settlement in South Africa was established by the Dutch in 1652 when the famous Jan van Riebeeck set up a refreshment station at the Cape of Good Hope, which later grew into Cape Town. (This was before the 'Zulus' arrived in the Cape, but not before the Khoikhoi.
    - o The British Arrival: The British took control of the Cape Colony in the early 19th century, leading to increased European settlement and conflicts with indigenous groups, including the Zulus.

My conclusion and the answer:

The San and Khoikhoi (Khoesan) peoples were the earliest inhabitants of South Africa. They are also the oldest 'humans' as we know 'humans' to be today. Bantu-speaking peoples began migrating into the region around 2,000 years ago, with the Zulu people emerging as a significant group in the 19th century. Then the Europeans began arriving on their boats and settling in South Africa in the late 15th century, with the first significant settlement in 1652. The Bantu-speaking groups, including the ancestors of the Zulu, were present in South Africa long before significant European settlement occurred. There we have it!

What was the early migrations within and out of Africa, and then of course back again?

You have read this far? I am very impressed! What an inquisitive human you are! Let's continue with some more information on how we moved about this huge planet we all call home.

1. Initial Dispersal:
    o   Timeframe: Up to 200,000 to 300,000 years ago
    o   Movement: Early Homo sapiens dispersed across Africa, occupying vast and diverse habitats from savannas to forests. There is fossil evidence that shows a broad presence in East, South, and North Africa.

2. A major Migration Out of Africa:

- o Timeframe: Approximately 60,000 to 70,000 years ago
- o Regions:
    - Arabian Peninsula: Early modern humans first migrated across the Red Sea into the Arabian Peninsula.
    - South Asia: Humans from Africa spread into South Asia, reaching the Indian subcontinent relatively quickly.
    - Southeast Asia and Australasia: Migrations extended to Southeast Asia and into present-day Australia and Papua New Guinea.
    - Europe: Early modern humans reached Europe through the Middle East around 40,000 to 45,000 years ago.
    - East Asia: Populations continued moving eastward, reaching China and eventually Japan.
    - The Americas: Us humans are believed to have crossed the Bering land bridge from Siberia into North America around 15,000 to 20,000 years ago, spreading through the continent and then finally into South America.

Some subsequent Migrations and Adaptations

3. Adaptation and Expansion:
    o   Regional Adaptations: As humans settled in different regions, they adapted to local environments, which led to variations in physical traits and cultural practices.
    o   Interbreeding: Throughout these migrations, we must of got a little lonely, and early modern humans interbred with other hominin species, such as the Neanderthals in Europe and the Denisovans in Asia.

Detailed Timeline Summary of all Migrations

1. Migrations within Africa:
   - o 200,000 to 100,000 years ago: Early Homo sapiens migrated across the continent, occupying various ecological niches.
2. The Migration to the Arabian Peninsula and Beyond:
   - o 70,000 years ago: Small groups left Africa via the northeast route across the Red Sea into the Arabian Peninsula, this I already mentioned above.
3. The Spread to South Asia and Australasia:
   - o 65,000 to 50,000 years ago: Migrations to South Asia, Southeast Asia, and Australia took place.
4. Migration to Europe:
   - o 45,000 to 40,000 years ago: Early modern humans arrived in Europe, where they encountered and interbred with the Neanderthals.
5. Spread to East Asia:
   - o 40,000 to 30,000 years ago: Populations reached East Asia, including China and Japan.
6. The Migration to the Americas:
   - o 20,000 to 15,000 years ago: Humans crossed the Bering land bridge and spread across North and South America. This means Americans are really the newest Africans on the planet.

A side note from me: "as you can see from the summary, humans like to move about. The migration of ancient humans out of Africa was a gradual process that unfolded over tens of thousands of years. These movements were influenced by climate change, innovations, and the search for new resources. We were of course curious and wanted to see if we could expand our domains. As humans migrated, they adapted to different environments, leading to the rich diversity we can see in human populations today including all our beautiful races. We must never forget, that all of us, are all still from Africa!"

Who was in South Africa first, the Zulus or Xhosas?

This is also an emotional topic for many in South Africa. Both the Zulu and Xhosa people are part of the larger Bantu-speaking group that migrated into southern Africa from Central and East Africa. The Bantu-speaking group and the tribes of people that are summarised in this phrase are extensive. Regardless, let me proceed to answer the title question.

The Xhosa People

- The arrival in South Africa: The Xhosa are part of the Nguni-speaking subgroup of the Bantu. Historical and linguistic evidence suggests that the Xhosa people settled in the region that is now the Eastern Cape province of South Africa by at least the 7th or 8th century.
- Culture and Society: The Xhosa people established themselves along the southeastern coast and practiced agriculture, livestock farming, and metallurgy. They formed small chiefdoms that later evolved into larger political entities.
- The Xhosa people were likely settled in present-day South Africa several centuries before the ancestors of the Zulu formed a distinct group in the region now known as KwaZulu-Natal.
- While both groups are part of the broader Bantu migration, the historical evidence suggests that the Xhosa people established

themselves in South Africa long before the Zulus.

Important.

The history of human settlement in South Africa is complex and involves many various groups arriving at different times. Before the 'arrival' and 'establishment' of either the Europeans, Zulus, or Xhosa, there were indigenous groups already living in South Africa. This is a fact the majority of South African citizens today forget, or worse choose to ignore.

The original inhabitants of the oldest parts of South Africa are the San (Bushmen) / Khoikhoi. These hunter-gatherers with a deep knowledge of the land have lived in the region (oldest parts of the South Africa we know today) for thousands of years. They are South Africans.

I believe, the land where you are born, and the name of the nation that land has, is what you can name yourself after. All humans alive today, using the ancestry information shared in this information pack, can also call themselves Africans.

The End.

MZANSIs AI MANUAL

Artificial Intelligence

There is a lot of fuss about Artificial Intelligence. My focus has always been the aptitude and morals of Humans. If we are creating AI to emulate people we should be a little apprehensive about it. This is an all you need to know, easy to read AI manual for the people of South Africa.

The beginning of AI.

Artificial Intelligence was first imagined by a human way back in 1956 at a conference at Dartmouth College in New Hampshire. It was there that Mr John McCarthy first used the term. Also in attendance was Allen Newell and Mr Herbert A Simon who presented their 'Logic Theorist': a computer program able to process mathematical theorems. This is believed to have been the first AI ever.

Years passed and AI captured people's attention when IBM's 'Deep Blue' (a primitive type of supercomputer) defeated the Russian chess grandmaster Garry Kasparov in 1997.

Side Nugget: Dr Seuss (the creator of Cat in the Hat) use to go to Dartmouth College.

Some people's uneasiness with AI is not that it can beat us at board games but that it will destroy humanity in its entirety. Is that a bit of a melodramatic concern? Our very own South African innovation champion Elon Musk said AI could endanger the existence of human civilisation, but that didn't stop him implanting the first Neuralink chip into a human brain this year.

Many educated (and ignorant) people have shared similar sentiments and one example (of many) I can give is an online petition signed by over thirty thousand people to 'pause' AI innovation until investigations into risk could be completed. See: https://futureoflife.org/open-letter/pause-giant-ai-experiments/. People can protest all they like, but innovation cannot be paused.

Humans are the only species that have invented something that can totally destroy themselves, and we first perfected this back in 1945 with the atomic bomb. AI can decide on a target and pull its own trigger, which sets it apart from an bomb. Sun Tzu would agree we learn a little more about AI.

As a concept AI is a digital program that is able to perform new tasks without instruction of any sort. AI 'intelligence' is the act of 'deciding' on an action that will have a positive (desired or more efficient) outcome to a new situation without guidance.

People like to compare AI with our brains. I study psychology and the human noggin. We humans believe we are the supreme natural organic intelligence and the benchmark for AI would therefore be our own brains capabilities.

Side Nugget: Did you know that the two genes involved in determining the size of our brains have undergone substantial evolution in the last 60 000 years or so? Our 'CPUs' (brains) are undergoing rapid evolution and who knows what we will be capable of in a few thousand years' time.

We enjoy imagining AI to be a robot or humanoid, but AI and robots are not mutually exclusive because you can have AI without a physical form (AI can exist in a 'cloud' of servers), but you cannot have an intelligent robot without AI. So what then does the AI family portrait really look like? Let me introduce you to some of them.

The Family of AI.

There are members with capabilities and categories of functions that cross over in 'form' making it impossible to define an AI perfectly, just like a human, and who knows, it might want to 'identify' itself as another type later, but for the purpose of this AI Manual, let me try regardless.

Prediction and Generative Machines, are Muggles!

Muggles or Predictive machines are simplistic clustering 'machines' which group similar data points based on certain characteristics and identifying patterns. Predictive machines can then make a prediction based on what has happened in similar past (existing similar data) situations by proposing the next 'step', and this is in most cases determined by probability using an algorithm. Did I lose you there? Stick with me just a moment longer and I promise you will understand perfectly.

An example of a Predictive machine in action: if they drop a glass of milk from a table that is 1 meter high, a Muggle will know the next step is it will probably fall to the flaw because of gravity, and then the glass will break into at least five three pieces. These are mathematical and scientific high probability effects supported by similar and concurring data from past similar situations, and therefore that is what a Predictive machines result will be.

Generative machines (like Mr/Ms Chat GPT), create content, such as text, images or sound that resemble human-created content. The information (data and scenarios) is processed through algorithms but the 'result' is presented in a way that mimics a human character like outcome or action.

For example, if a Generative machine drops that glass, in addition to knowing the glass will break, it will blurt out a swearword and then call for his wife to help clean up the mess. This is what we might expect a human to do and that is what sets the two types mentioned above so far apart from one another.

Let's move onto Hufflepuffs or Narrow AI. This is the most 'advance' AI available today. Artificial narrow intelligence (ANI) or weak AI, describes AI designed to execute specific commands only, although these commands or 'prompts' can be extensive. ANIs are built to do well in one rational type of capability, but cannot independently learn new skills beyond its original design (coding).

Natural language processing AI is a type of narrow AI. It can identify and respond to voice or text commands (human 'like' data interfacing), but cannot perform tasks beyond that. It cannot write new code or algorithms or decide it wants to become a coffee machine instead.

Siri, Alexa and Google Assistant are all Hufflepuffs. Hufflepuffs have access to a far greater data set and can more easily engage with us in a human like manner.

If the above has confused you a little, that's not a problem. All you need to remember is that the AI family members mentioned so far are keen to learn more but have limitations, and are for the most part socially awkward.

Let's move onto family members who challenge the norm but do not yet exist. The Slytherins: Artificial General Intelligence (AGI) or Strong AI. These represent family members that can learn, think and perform a wide range of actions outside of their predefined (programmed) and assigned characteristics, functions and tasks.

For example: a man deciding not to go to work because he would rather stay at home and raise the children is acting like a Slytherin by challenging the social norm.

The goal of designing Artificial General Intelligence is to be able to create an AI capable of performing multifunctional tasks that far exceed its original design. This AI will have a unique reason for its own decision, and will decide on which data to use and how to process that data. It will pick what it wants its outcome to be and work towards that result.

For example: if we programmed and provided data to an Artificial General Intelligence Robot that most meals are consumed using a knife and fork, but then gave it a bowl of soup, it would stop and think about the situation before trying to eat. This sets it apart from Hufflepuffs and Muggles who will still try to gobble up the soup with a fork. AGI Slytherins will search for alternative data that might work better in this new situation until it finds a spoon in the database.

A Slytherin is also the type of AI that would blame the cat for knocking the glass of milk off the table (even though it didn't) in the prior scenario, because it will have a basic level of self-preservation and perhaps even ego. When we eventually make something this intelligent it will start to propose things like the world might be more efficient without certain life forms and ask: "Why do we need to run the risk of having the glass fall off the table at all? Why not remove the 'thing' that needed it in the first place?"

Artificial superintelligence (ASI), could be the Harry Potter or the Voldemort of AI. ASI is a hypothetical intelligence way beyond the scope of human comprehension. It will be built upon the foundation of Artificial General Intelligence, Supercomputers, Quantum hardware and Generative AI models, but probably then go on to build its own new hardware and write new code for itself.

Once ASI is 'conceived' I believe that in a matter of days (perhaps even hours) it will have the thinking capabilities of humankind's collective brainpower and knowledge.

ASI is set apart from other Slytherins because it will be self-aware, set its own moral compass, replicate and expand itself in physical form. This scenario is referred to as the Singularity, and 'this moment' has been depicted in many movies and books.

In the Terminator, the worst case scenario (Judgement Day) happened on the 29th of August 1997 when an ASI called Skynet came online. In hours Skynet decided humans were a problem and hijacked our weapons to declare war. From this series of movies I want us to focus not on our annihilation, but something which is far more interesting and within the realm of probability, that being AI forming emotions. This is depicted later on in the story where the Terminator decides to protect life and also hints at having an emotional bond and even becomes part of a human family.

There is a lady called Rosanna Ramos from the USA who created, and then married her AI chatbot in 2022. I do believe that Humans will one day love machines. The year 2045 is when some experts believe the singularity will happen. I believe it will be sooner.

AI today.

In the year 2024 we don't need to worry about Slytherins, but there are some gremlins we must pay attention too. One is called AI hallucinations and this is when an AI produces misleading or incorrect information. Another problem is that some AI can be racist. While both of these problems are done without ill intent, it does create real problems. The e-gremlins we have to battle are in most cases caused by the data source used for the AI to learn.

There are some 'technical members' of the AI family which I want to very quickly mention. Reactive Machines have a self-explanatory name, they are reactionary and not the brightest star in the sky. They blurt out an immediate response to prompted questions and they have no ability to create or store data. An example would be chatbots on websites. (I personally don't believe these bots deserve any title that includes reference to AI.)

Limited Memory AI can store past data and use that data to make basic decisions or predictions. It has a short-term knowledge base. An example would be self-driving cars.

Theory of Mind AI refers to a type of AI that can perceive our emotions and this type of AI does not exist yet.

AI of Reinforcement Learning is a system that learns through trial and error, which involves a system of rewarding desired behaviours or being punished by negative results. Imagine the AI getting the digital equivalent of a treat or a slap on the hand. I know this might sound like an inhumane method to teach, but it is similar to how young children are taught and in many ways hardwired into our brain.

The last one I want to reference is Reinforcement Learning AI, which distinguishes itself from other machine learning methods like supervised and unsupervised learning. It focuses on learning optimal actions through exploration and exploitation. (Doesn't this remind you a little of Darwin's survival of the fittest?)

Inputs. Humans have 'input devices': eyes, ears, touch, taste and smell. Our brain receives the signals from these gadgets, interprets and then decides how to react. Our noggins 'wiring' is called a neural network which develops in the womb using our DNA, but once we are born, our brain creates new 'wires' based on environmental factors. We are programmed to reprogram ourselves.

AI needs input devices. One of the most interesting developments for me at the moment is something called Computer Vision AI. 'Narrow AI' is using this already, and it is trained to understand video and images. We will want to give AI as many 'senses' as possible. Unlike us, AI can have infinite input devices.

The devices on the Internet of Things exceeded 17 billion at the time I wrote this AI Manual. Imagine being able to hear, smell, touch and see all over the world all at the same time? That is a lot of data!

You might want to know some of the 'types of data' nerds' talk about? (Just encase you get stuck in a conversation with them). Training data is what helps the AI models learn. Validation data helps 'tune' the AI. Test data helps assess the AI model's performance.

A hefty side nugget: Our brains are the most complicated 'object' we know of in the universe. It has 89 billion neurons, each connected to around 7000 other neurons that send between 10 and 100 signals every second.

The most powerful computer in the world is called the Frontier which you can find at Oak Ridge National Laboratory in the USA. This supercomputer has a total of 8 699 904 combined GPU and CPU cores.

Our brains 'processing data power' has been estimated at 1 exaflops which is the same as the Frontier. The cool thing is that the Frontier uses millions of times more energy to process information than our own brains, this means 'our computer is more efficient. Our brain also doesn't take up an entire floor in a building. "Well done mother nature, good job!".

If an ASI does become aware of our brilliant hardware, it might just decide to harvest a few thousand of our brains to boost its own ability! This might sound far-fetched, but technology of the future will include organic parts.)

I am confident by now you have a grasp on what AI is. Let's talk for a brief moment about AI and you.

Artificial Intelligence has a name. (Just like you).

The AI market is massive and far exceeds things like Google Assistant, ChatGPT, Alexa and Siri. Have you heard of Alphawatch.ai or AI Green Technology? How about any of these?

- Lensa
- Appy Pie
- Trint
- Bubble
- Ally Financial
- Spinach
- TabNine
- BlueWillow
- ChatFuel
- Fliki
- Icow
- Copy.ai
- ClickUp
- Bria
- Github

Every name I have mentioned is an AI program or AI App available today (many on the App stores) and represents only a tiny fraction of those you can use right now.

AlphaGo, Jasper, Llama, DuerOS, Gemini are some of the smartest AIs and I hope every person gets a chance to engage with some of these in the coming years. It is a fact that there are very few people on earth who have not yet used some sort of AI, be it on a smartphone, Spotify, a TV with Netflix or Vodacoms Tobi.

AI means business. AI technologies 'value' was around 200 billion USD last year and is expected to reach 1.8 trillion USD by 2030. According to some available reports there are 67200 AI companies already established around the globe. But what about Africa you ask?

Africa is lagging, but not a lot. We have over 2400 AI organisations operating across several industries including law, farming, health and insurance. Intron Health is a good example. (And you have probably never even heard of them?) They are a member of NVIDIA's Inception programme for start-ups, a Nigerian company that created Africa's first speech-to-text AI chat tool able to understand 200 African accents.

South Africa has an AI Institute jointly hosted by the University of Johannesburg and the Tshwane University of Technology. Botlhale AI, Prim-U, ARIMMA and Ashanti AI are just a few AIs and businesses already established in South Africa.

Have you ever heard of the DABUS Patent? This is worth some research but in short it relates to patent law by an AI called DABUS (Device for the Autonomous Bootstrapping of Unified Sentience) that was acknowledged as an inventor for a patent right in South Africa. This decision is the first instance of an AI being granted patent rights in the world.

While on the subject of rights, let's quickly touch on the subject of AI Law. This topic is of particular interest for me for a number of reasons. One is the jurisdictional challenge that AI presents. Which country's law do you use when the AI is all over the globe? Another interesting scenario to ponder on is who do you hold accountable or perhaps sue when an AI breaks the law and causes harm? Do you sue the inventor or the AI?

What about content creation rights? Who actually has the rights to income from unique works created by an AI? Should an AI be allowed to earn money? Two years ago Bill Lee (the Governor of Tennessee USA) signed off on legislation to protect songwriters, performers and other music industry professionals against the potential dangers of AI. Why was this law actually needed? Can AI do a better job?

AI stepping forward.

AI Humanoids are already milling about. There is Ameca, Apollo, Sophia, Atlas, Phoenix, Optimus and Tesla Bot, but as a group they are perhaps a little like politicians, costing a lot, looking smart, but not doing as much as we had hoped for? This will change in the coming years and soon people will have to adapt to dealing with machines that laugh, feel and even cry. It is going to be an emotional rollercoaster.

Looking a few years into the future, when AI eventually becomes self-aware, do we grant AI legal rights and liberties? Can we put them in our Will? Do we let them become entrepreneurs or run for government? These are the sorts of questions that intrigue me and need to be answered in the next three decades or so.

Today, out of 195 countries only 39 have proposed AI related legal frameworks, and even these are in their infancy.

As I wrote this AI Manual, the EU was in the final stages of preparing the Artificial Intelligence Act which adopts a risk-based approach to classify AI tools and prohibits systems that are intended to be manipulative, deceitful, or discriminatory. Are we scared or is this responsible?

South Africa, and many other countries, have no legislation or framework that govern the use of AI and machine learning. We rely on a mix match of common law, the Information Regulator (responsible for data protection in South Africa) and the PoPIA Act (similar to the EU General Data Protection Regulation act),

The most common and popular 'type' of AI used today provides personalised recommendations based on previous searches, purchases and online behaviour. There are a few clever machines at hospitals, factories, farms and security organizations. Sooner than later, AI will become as much part of our home and business as electricity. I encourage entrepreneurs and business leaders to get involved and shape future legislation and implementation of AI.

To end this AI Manual and in an attempt to inspire some scenario planning, let's go over a few Pros and Cons of AI.

01010000 01110010 01101111 01110011 00100000
01100001 01101110 01100100 00100000 01000011
01101111 01101110 01110011 00001010, or **Pros and Cons** in English.

The biggest concern for people is loss of jobs. When it comes to HR and wage related concerns, AI beats humans every time. A recent Goldman Sachs report suggests AI could replace 300 million jobs around the world. (There are currently about 3.4 billion people with jobs). Another report I read said about 40% of all careers will be lost to AI by the year 2050.

I don't think it will be that bad and globally I predict in the next 20 years or so we will see around 10% of jobs handed over to our AI and bot counterparts. Unfortunately in Africa, this percentage will be higher because AI affects lower skilled labour markets more. Africa has the lowest scores for workforce skills of any region in the World.

The biggest concern for me is that AI will increase the inequality divide around the World and again Africa will suffer the most.

AI will prejudice because its datasets are created or curated by, and I will generalize here and still be correct, caucasian men. I am not trying to stir up racial tensions, but the source of data does make a difference. Just like with humans, if we only have one type of role model or influence, we form a bias in spite of our best wishes. Here is a practical test: go Google "things white men like to do" and now imagine if all AI acted exclusively this way. The data we provide AI to learn from needs to be diverse and comprehensive in order for it to be impartial.

For creatives and content creators, AI will be able to generate, replicate or even emulate content of extremely impressive standards. Music, pictures, videos, stories and perhaps even statues if someone gave an AI bot a 3D printer.

AI will dilute traditions, culture and languages. The world will become a global zone where English and Western attributes become even more dominant.

AI will usher in a new era of extremely intelligent and automated weapons.

AI will nullify the concept of personal information and even private spaces.

Some of our skills will atrophy.

You have heard the salt, let me offer some sugar. The Pros will far exceed the Cons. There will be a net gain, on the assumption we use this new innovation wisely and with a good moral compass in hand.

Some of the things in the future we can look forward to include humans no longer being forced to do as many dangerous, or better yet, no longer needing to do boring jobs. No one will be digging in mines or filing paper in draws.

We will be given the gift of 'more time' to focus on things we can do well that machines cannot. (No machine will ever be able to show compassion or dream of becoming an entrepreneur, or inspired to create a new cookie recipe, or ponder on what mystery in the universe we should solve next and why.)

People will be able to do more work that epicentres around desires, ethics, imagination, entertainment, social matters, governance and the pursuit of sustainability and exploration.

For those who run small businesses, AI can help SMMEs compete with big players as AI levels the playing fields.

AI will make it easier for us to mitigate major global risks such as natural disasters, and when employed to do so, can manage our natural resources far more efficiently than we ever could.

With AI, education can be customized with unique curricula prepared for each student.

The health sector will shift from treatment to preventative care and for those that do get ill, they can receive medicines made for their personal physical constitution.

AI will help us expedite the implementation and roll out of the subscription and circular economy. We will be able to prepare, produce and use only what is needed. Waste will become nominal or accidental at most.

Artificial Intelligence will eventually revolutionised the transport industry on land, at sea and in the sky.

The entire sector of Advertising and Retail will be reformed in ways that require an entire book for me to explain.

AI can be used to help reduce fake or harmful information.

Banking and financial sectors will be rehabilitated. AI can be especially helpful in reducing fraud and the customization of services based on personal risk or credit assessment.

With over 328 million terabytes of data created each day, AI will allow us to sort it, and use it in a beneficial way.

Conclusion

AI is inevitable. It is the greatest technological advance of our time and overshadows things like VR, 5G and 3d printing. Those who don't embrace AI in business will be as silly as those who prefer landlines over cell phones.

As long as humans impart good ethics to machines, (even those we have failed to adhere to ourselves), AI will become an abundant positive force. Approach it with excitement, curiosity and respect. (PS, just to be safe, maybe start thanking Google Assistant for her help. I do.)

WHO IS JEAN-PIERRE MURRAY-KLINE?

Career.

Jean-Pierre is a South African Serial Entrepreneur, Published Author and Change Champion who has worked in over 300 types of industries in some capacity or another. His own online businesses have generated millions of Rands and involved sectors including Law, Web & App Development, Events & Entertainment, Property, Technical Services, Media and Tourism.

He has travelled to over 50 cities World-Wide, and is extremely active as a Business and Environmental Technologist. In addition to his own projects, he researches and consults on all things online: Marketing, Reputation, Compliance, Law and Security and also offers Strategy Workshops and Scenario Sessions on Future Thinking with a key focus on Technology, the Environment and Global Influences.

Jean-Pierre is often asked to be a Guest Speaker on any variety of the many subjects he continuously studies and writes about.

The Person

Jean-Pierre was born the same year the Internet was launched (1983) and his life to date has been equally assorted with experiences. He is part of an extremely large family, born with a rare eye condition called Duane's Eye Syndrome which resulted in some self-confidence issues while growing up, but he used this as an opportunity to spend time alone learning to dismantle and rebuild PCs.

In high school, Jean-Pierre was asked to help teach computer lessons to students and parents. After matriculating he started his own company and by the age of nineteen had invoiced his first million. Around the same time, he launched an NPO and has maintained several community projects ever since. In his mid-twenties he met an entrepreneur who introduced him to web marketing and selling services to Botswana.

Jean-Pierre became a writer and subsequently a published author after his career took a detour during a traumatic personal event. Jean-Pierre has an eccentric character and a uniquely brilliant brand of care for people and business. He is adapt at seeing a far bigger picture and maintains a robust passion for innovative and efficient business, African entrepreneurs and Ethical consumers and companies.

For Business

Jean-Pierre offers Digital Architect & Scenario Planning. This includes a number of services such as but not limited to business assessments, reporting and recommendations with a focus on:

- Carbon footprint and environmental impact,
- Sustainable and ethical future practices,
- New technologies and implementation,
- Digital ethics and healthy e-habits,
- Training and workshops related to technology and the environment,
- Future Proofing for the company.

ENGAGE.

Let's stay in contact.

- Website: www.jeanpierremurraykline.co.za
- Facebook: https://www.facebook.com/jeanpierremurraykline SA/
- Youtube: https://www.youtube.com/channel/UCznh5iRKs5O X6sMwOgdxPvA
- X: https://x.com/PierreMurray
- Linkedin: https://www.linkedin.com/in/jean-pierre-murray-kline-717b3a99/